THE BOOK OF THE

BRITANNIA PACIFICS

A Pictorial Accompaniment

Notes by Ian Sixsmith

70000 BRITANNIA on the London Midland, at Crewe in May 1963. *The Book of the Britannias,* naturally, concerns itself greatly with the noble art of 'engine picking', tracing the numerous and fascinating detail variations exhibited on the 'Brits.' throughout their all-too short lives. This is one in thoroughly 'late BR' condition – second totem on tender, AWS battery box on running plate, handholds instead of handrails on smoke deflectors, electrification flashes and other modifications that appeared over the years. Photograph D.W. Winkworth.

IRWELL PRESS Ltd.

Front Cover Photograph Upper: A Polmadie pairing
at Carlisle. 70050 as yet without a name, alongside
45556 NOVA SCOTIA on 26 August 1954.
Photograph James Stevenson, courtesy Hamish
Stevenson.

Front Cover Photograph Lower: In the sparkling
condition that characterised much of the two
Britannias' time on the Southern, IRON DUKE
on the Arrow at Tonbridge in August 1954. Usual
exotic SR lamp iron arrangement. Photograph
Ted's Dad.

First published in the United Kingdom in 2004
by Irwell Press Limited, 59A, High Street, Clophill,
Bedfordshire MK45 4BE
Printed by Interprint

The Golden One. WILLIAM SHAKESPEARE in its shimmering Festival of Britain finish, taking water at Stewarts Lane shed on 2 April 1955 and at Dover in August 1956, in the company of 30798 and 34091 just out of view to the right. Photographs A.R. Carpenter and J. Robertson, The Transport Treasury.

An Easter Saturday at Cambridge, 4 April 1953, epitomising the GE Britannia revolution – Norwich's 70013 OLIVER CROMWELL waits while Stratford's 70041 SIR JOHN MOORE backs down on to the London train. Photograph M.N. Bland, The Transport Treasury.

THE BOOK OF THE BRITANNIAS
A Pictorial Accompaniment

Picture This

Over the last seven years or so the Irwell Press 'Book Of' locomotive studies has covered many of the principal express classes. Some have been reprinted while others are out of print; others remain to be reprinted. Beginning in 1997 they have been:

The Book of the BR Standards
The Book of the Coronation Pacifics
The Book of the Royal Scots
The Book of the Merchant Navy Pacifics
The Book of the Jubilee 4-6-0s
The Book of the West Country/Battle of Britain Pacifics
The Book of the Princess Royal Pacifics
The Book of the Patriot 4-6-0s
The Book of the BR Standards: 2
The Book of the A3 Pacifics
The Book of the Britannias

The idea of this *Pictorial Accompaniment* is to serve up a wider range of photographs for the particular classes covered and this first one, for the Britannias will, it is hoped, presage further efforts directed at some of the other classes covered so far. It accompanies, supplements and complements the latest 'Book Of', *The Book of the Britannias* by Richard Derry.

****

There have been endless writings concerning the Britannia Pacifics, not least in earlier Irwell Press publications (*Britannia: Birth of a Locomotive, The Book of the BR Standards, The Book of the BR Standards: 2* and *Rule Britannia!*) and many other publications have dealt with these famous Pacifics, sometimes in enormous detail. Commonly ascribed to Riddles, the Britannias (as well as other BR Standards, particularly the 9F 2-10-0s) the 'true architect' was his third in command, E.S. Cox.

It was the economic weakness of Britain in the post-war years (which were also the first years of the newly nationalised British Railways) which determined the further construction of steam and, in particular, the BR Standard range. Steam was cheap to build, from materials which largely avoided imports (though perennial 'steel shortages' saw some Britannias postponed) in their manufacture. Good, cheap, coal was getting dearer even if there was an inexhaustible supply still in the ground and diesels and electrics were increasingly viable. Yet such a conversion meant buying from the United States – expending precious dollars and then more dollars for the fuel. It was for these reasons that Cox and Riddles gave us one last generation of steam locomotives. The nuts and bolts of the story are of course contained in *The Book of the Britannias* so only some short notes will follow here (we want you to buy Richard Derry's 'Book Of' too, after all!)

The Britannias could be said to have grown out of the famous 'Initial Report' of June 1948, even as the Locomotive Exchanges were under way. This proposed twelve types, in three main categories; the first of these three was entitled 'entirely new designs' – the

The lady glides, barely noticed, through the outskirts of Ipswich back in the middle 1950s. By this time the GE Section timetabling revolution was complete – the one and only time a major service had been entirely recast to suit a new class of steam locomotive.

Britannias of course, together with a heavy freight loco. At first this was conceived as a 2-8-2 rather than the 2-10-0 we eventually saw.

****

BRITANNIA was named by the Minister of Transport at Marylebone station on 30 January 1951. Sir Eustace Missenden, Chairman of the Railway Executive, presided and declared that such events indicated that British Railways were 'pressing forward despite difficulties'. The new locomotive would give 'maximum locomotive availability and minimum cost of coal and maintenance over a greater range of railway routes than was ever previously possible with a single design'. Its preliminary trials 'had suggested every prospect of realising the economies and increased efficiency, and so of improving further upon the reduction in coal consumption which they were already obtaining.' BRITANNIA was 'physical evidence of the creative work performed by British Railways'. He unveiled the magnificent nameplate (how fortunate that the plan to call it Lord Hurcomb after the Chairman of the Executive was abandoned) on the smoke deflector of

No.70000. The Pacific, shockingly new to many, then glided off to its Stratford home in stately fashion and the story of the Britannias (now underway once more with 70013 at the National Railway Museum and a possible 're-birth' of 70000) had begun.

I would like to thank Eric Youldon, Richard Derry, Bryan Wilson and Richard Hardy in compiling this pictorial.

Below. BRITANNIA near Stratford shed on 20 April 1957. It has come up on the Hook Continental (460-470 tons) and was in fact the regular engine from 1951 to 1959/60, effectively outbased at Parkeston (these allocations never showed on the Engine Histories) but worked by Stratford men. 70000 is either waiting or already drifting down to the Carriage Shed. A.E. Bennett, The Transport Treasury.

Bottom right. The second 'Brit.', 70001 LORD HURCOMB with an up train at Ipswich early on in its life. It is not in precisely original condition by any means; it has the larger dome fitted after the early water carry-over problems, the 'flexible screens' have appeared and the mechanical lubricator cover plate is off. Note the BR1 tender with its low collector dome; on the BR1A it was markedly higher. As yet, the tender footstep bracket has not appeared. Photograph James Stevenson, courtesy Hamish Stevenson.

Above. BRITANNIA on the London Midland again (see page i) but a GE engine, at Lichfield on 7 May 1953. It had had two visits to Crewe, a Light Intermediate and a Non-Classified, though it should have been back in East Anglia by now. Compare with the first picture – original tender totem, earlier front smokebox steps, original deflector handrails. It goes on... Photograph The Transport Treasury.

70002 GEOFFREY CHAUCER waiting on shed at Stratford, 7 June 1959. This is after the transfer of the Stratford Britannias (to ease their maintenance) to Norwich – something which took place early in 1959, not 1958 as is so often stated. Behind 70002 lies the rubble that had been part of the Jubilee shed, now in process of conversion to a diesel depot. Much has been written of the lime scaling on the Britannias, often draped from the whistle on the smokebox and all over the cylinder casing, as here. It is always ascribed to priming but R.H.N. Hardy, who was at Stratford during this time, doubts this all-too frequent verdict: 'Above the cylinders and hidden by a removable cover was an anti-vacuum or snifting valve from which steam often used to dribble down the cylinder casing when the engine was standing with the regulator closed. If the regulator is open, the valve is closed as it is when the engine is coasting on a short cut-off. If the whistle valve was blowing through slightly, the same happens on the smokebox side and it soon turns white if left uncleaned for any length of time. The effect of dribbling steam and water when standing in steam inside the shed for several hours was only too evident and, on an engine such as 70004 at Stewarts Lane, had to be rigorously cleaned daily. It was not a sign of priming and it was rare for a 7MT to prime. I cannot recall it happening when I was travelling on the footplate during the period 1952-1961.' Photograph Frank Hornby.

Engine Picking the Britannias – A Brief Guide

The Britannias appeared in three batches, all from Crewe Works:

70000 (5/1/51) to 70024 (6/10/51). Order No.E479, 1951 Programme authorised 17/11/49.
70025 (15/9/52) to 70044 (4/6/53). Order No.E483, 1952 Programme authorised 4/1/51.
70045 (16/6/54) to 70054 (13/9/54). Order No.E486, 1953 programme authorised 29/11/51 but delayed due to steel shortage.

Nos.70000-70014 cost £20,025 each, increasing to £22,734 for Nos.70025-70029.

After that the price dipped several times by a few hundred pounds until Nos.70045-70049, which cost £24,837. The last ten with BR1D tenders, Nos.70050-70054, cost £25,331.

Names
70000 BRITANNIA
70001 LORD HURCOMB
70002 GEOFFREY CHAUCER
70003 JOHN BUNYAN
70004 WILLIAM SHAKESPEARE
70005 JOHN MILTON
70006 ROBERT BURNS

70007 COEUR-DE-LION
70008 BLACK PRINCE
70009 ALFRED THE GREAT
70010 OWEN GLENDOWER
70011 HOTSPUR
70012 JOHN OF GAUNT
70013 OLIVER CROMWELL
70014 IRON DUKE
70015 APOLLO
70016 ARIEL
70017 ARROW
70018 FLYING DUTCHMAN
70019 LIGHTNING
70020 MERCURY

70021	MORNING STAR
70022	TORNADO
70023	VENUS
70024	VULCAN
70025	WESTERN STAR
70026	POLAR STAR
70027	RISING STAR
70028	ROYAL STAR
70029	SHOOTING STAR
70030	WILLIAM WORDSWORTH
70031	BYRON
70032	TENNYSON
70033	CHARLES DICKENS
70034	THOMAS HARDY
70035	RUDYARD KIPLING
70036	BOADICEA
70037	HEREWARD THE WAKE
70038	ROBIN HOOD
70039	SIR CHRISTOPHER WREN
70040	CLIVE OF INDIA
70041	SIR JOHN MOORE
70042	LORD ROBERTS
70043	LORD KITCHENER
70044	EARL HAIG
70045	LORD ROWALLAN
70046	ANZAC
70047	
70048	THE TERRITORIAL ARMY 1908-1958
70049	SOLWAY FIRTH
70050	FIRTH OF CLYDE
70051	FIRTH OF FORTH
70052	FIRTH OF TAY
70053	MORAY FIRTH
70054	DORNOCH FIRTH

This *Pictorial Accompaniment* to *The Book of the Britannias* is just that, and it is not the intention to provide the full story of design, experience in traffic, modifications, tests and accidents; all that is dealt with in *The Book of the Britannias* by Richard Derry. As for the *full* panoply of Britannia variations, we've cunningly arranged that you'll need 'The Book Of' itself. However, here is a very brief summary (very brief it must be emphasised) of the visual differences (usually highlighted in the captions) to look out for:

Brake Hose Pipes: Upright pipes on the first twenty or so gave way to a type which projected forward. The first ones were then modified to match.

Lamp Brackets: The pattern of lamp irons changed and varied to accommodate (broadly speaking):
GE Section discs
Southern discs and lamps
WR lamps
Safety considerations once under the wires on the LMR

Driving Wheel Axles: The coupled wheels of the first twenty-five engines had hollow axles, altered to solid in the light of the wheel shift problems experienced on the Britannias in 1951.

Bearings: Roller bearings characterised the new Pacifics though some were turned out with plain bearings. The plain bearing trailing

axleboxes on 70040-70049 are clear to see externally.

Coupling Rods: Coupling rods were fluted on the first batch of Britannias, 70000-70024, but damage consequent on the axle shifting episode in 1951 meant they were superseded by tapered rectangular section ones. This new rectangular type was fitted from new to the later engines, 70025 onwards, but by no means all the first batch got the rectangular rods as they were supposed to. Some Britannias ended up with a mix of both; the fluted version had a habit of rearing its ugly head.

Sanding: 70000-70024 had TWO sandbox fillers each side, one in front of the middle axle, the second aft. The fillers were originally flush with the running plate on 70000-70024 but were later raised in most cases. 70025-70029 were raised from the first. The rest, 70030-70054, had THREE sandbox fillers each side, two front and aft

70003 JOHN BUNYAN at Cambridge on 19 May 1957 with an up train, moving slowly into the Cambridge platform. Flexible screens, front footstep and the higher buffer beam lamp irons of the Great Eastern Section. They were fitted for the discs that were used by day, though you have to get your eye in to spot the difference. Photograph R.C. Riley, The Transport Treasury.

6

70004 WILLIAM SHAKESPEARE at Victoria in September 1955. When it came to lamp irons there was nothing like the Southern – not only were its 'Brits.' fitted with those two extravagantly lengthy traditional SR irons but two more were fitted on the deflector stays. Note two sand fillers and rear coupling rod still fluted. There is a good view of the lubricator drive rod, running vertically down from the lubricator: this is the 'long' version. Photograph D.W. Winkworth.

WILLIAM SHAKESPEARE, now an LMR engine, out in Hertfordshire or Buckinghamshire with the Willesden breakdown train in the early 1960s, its 'Exhibition Finish' a very distant memory. Many Britannias had spells at Willesden and all must have visited the shed during their lives; 70004 was no exception and was there for three separate periods in the 1960s. A good view of the low BR1 collector dome – surprisingly the tender still carries the pre-1957 totem (it has been said that it retained it as late as 1963, though this seems unlikely) and if the view was clearer we'd see the four bolts for the Golden Arrow midway between the nameplate and the running plate. Photograph The Transport Treasury.

of the middle axle and a third ahead of the front drivers. Not much of all this is obvious in most views.

Mechanical Lubricators: One each side, they were hidden behind a bolted cover in the 'lip' of the running plate of the first Britannias. The covers were abandoned for ease of maintenance after a year or so.

Return Crank: Another change that took place while the class was in service concerned the return crank; originally mounted on a square pin, LNER style, from the mid-1950s it was gradually replaced by a standard LMS-type four stud design.

Liveries: The new 70000 appeared in plain black in early January 1951; within a week or two it had been repainted ready for naming in the lined dark green that was to become standard. Orange and black lining was applied on the boiler bands, cab and tender sides with only orange lining on the running plate and cylinders. The tender carried the first, lion and wheel totem; the later totem came in from March 1957, though a 'preview' had taken place the previous year, 1956, when 70016 ARIEL was unveiled with it and proclaimed 'the first engine in the whole fleet' (they meant *all* engines) to have it. The 1960s saw a few outshopped in plain green though 70013 OLIVER CROMWELL as the last steam engine overhauled at Crewe did emerge fully lined out.

No.70000 and, later, some others got a white painted cab roof for Royal Train

duties. 70004 carried the special 'Exhibition' chrome finish from the Festival of Britain.

Regulator Operating Rodding: The outside rodding to the smokebox steam regulator, it was found, lacked a certain rigidity! Support brackets were introduced half-way along the rods, firstly on the leading one and later to a lesser extent on the trailing rod.

Dome Cover: Early on, BRITANNIA and others experienced water carry-over which led to the introduction of a larger dome, duly applied to those in service or under construction at the time. Thereafter the larger dome was fitted to all new examples.

Speedometers: These did not appear on the first batch, 70000-70024 but thereafter they were increasingly common. A number of the early ones were subsequently fitted; moreover, although not all the second batch, 70025-70044, were fitted from new, all of the third batch, 70045-70054, *did* have them from new. In later years, some were removed!

ATC/AWS: Recognisable from the battery box on the running plate and protector plate behind the front drawhook on the right-hand side, the location of the reservoir cylinders remains a mystery (though 70048 did get them in the conventional place at least). Automatic Warning System was some years in the future when the Britannias came out but those destined for the Western Region got the local ATC (Automatic Train Control) at Swindon when delivered. AWS began to

appear on the non-WR engines from 1959 but in the end not all were fitted. The WR ATC gear was removed before the locos left the Western Region and some of them got the BR gear once on the LMR.

Smokebox Footsteps: The two small footsteps directly under the smokebox when the locomotives were new proved inadequate for fitting headboards to the top lamp bracket on the smokebox door. They were replaced from 1955 onwards by a single large plate between the frames, to a varying pattern – again, see photographs.

Smoke Deflectors: After the Milton accident of 1955 the order went out to remove the smoke deflector handrails and replace them by round handholds of the sort found on LMR 7P 4-6-0s and Duchess Pacifics. The Western chose rectangular cutouts instead. After a while the other Regions gave up and several 'Brits.' went to their end retaining the original 'dangerous' handrails.

Lubricator Drive Rod: This vertical rod operating the lubricator varied in length between engines and even on individual engines. They changed, seemingly indiscriminately, during works visits.

Draught Excluding: Famously, on the Britannias the whole of the cab floor was attached to the engine, so that the traditional fall-plate between engine and tender was done away with. There was a 'pillar handrail' from the rear of the cab roof to the extended

70005 JOHN MILTON, barely visible amid all its outpourings, makes to leave Ipswich for Liverpool Street with a train from Cromer High in the early 1950s. No 'flexible screen' or footstep on the tender yet; fluted rear coupling rod. The coming of the Britannias transformed the GE Section. As early as 1951, with yet more 7Ps still to come, locals accustomed to nothing grander than a 'Sandringham' were astonished to be treated to thirty trains a day hauled by ten different Pacifics. Photograph E.A. Elias, The Transport Treasury.

cab floor and the doors were contained within them. As has been well documented, a powerful backdraught could be blown backwards through the cab together with coal dust from the tender front and other points where it might have built up. Rubberised canvas 'flexible screens' were provided, to variable good effect. The last ten, with the BR1D tender and modified cab, were unaffected by all this.

Air Brakes: Air brakes were fitted to 70043 and 70044 when new, for trials between 1952 and 1955. Afterwards the gear was removed from both locomotives and the usual smoke deflectors were fitted together with nameplates.

Tenders: The first batch, 70000-70024, as well as 70030-70044, had the familiar *BR1*, water capacity 4,250 gallons and up to 7 tons of coal. Those in between, 70025-70029, had the modified version denoted *BR1A*. Internal alterations gave a water capacity of 5,000 gallons. There was also a larger pick-up dome on the rear. The last ten, 70045-70054, got high sided LM-style tenders, the *BR1D* with up to nine tons of coal – or even ten at a pinch. They were equipped with coal pushers Stanier Pacific-style.

The sloping top edge of the BR1 and 1A tenders were hazardous when men were directing the water bag and a foot step bracket was added to give a safer, flat surface. The first twenty-five, apart inevitably from one or two which took a while longer, were soon modified. The rest were built with the plates in place.

There were a number of tender changes and all of this, like much else, is examined in detail by Richard Derry in *The Book of the Britannias*.

70006 ROBERT BURNS with The Broadsman on Brentwood Bank, 26 June 1954. The GE Britannias were worked hard with many of the diagrams providing for prodigious daily mileages. The regular interval Liverpool Street-Norwich service on the Colchester main line was inaugurated on 2 July 1951 and the fastest times to Ipswich were better even than the prestige lightweight six coach streamlined 'East Anglian' of pre-war memory. 70006 came to the fore early on on the GE, running dynamometer car tests in June 1951 as a prelude to the new schedules. Photograph R. Wilson, The Transport Treasury.

10

The Broadsman again, behind Norwich 'Brit.' 70007 COEUR-DE-LION leaving Liverpool Street on 4 October 1956. In true 'best laid plans' fashion, the Liverpool Street turntable required attention in the weeks leading up to the introduction of the regular interval service and it was not possible in the 'lead-up' period for Norwich engines to work the best planned diagrams. Once the turntable was ready, from the first week in June 1951 (before the full inauguration on 2 July) B1s disappeared off the Norwich jobs and the full dramatic possibilities of the new Pacifics was apparent. Would anyone dare to model that bent deflector handrail? Photograph R.C. Riley, The Transport Treasury.

70007 COEUR-DE-LION in later guise, a Kingmoor engine at Perth with vans around 1964. It has the final generation of lamp irons – top one moved to side of smokebox door and 'middle' one on buffer beam shifted to align with it. This was a safety measure, to avoid firemen stretching up with a lamp under the 25kV wires. Photograph The Transport Treasury.

70008 BLACK PRINCE with the down Broadsman (low headboard) entering Ipswich in the early days of 7P working. It is worth pointing out that the main line from London to Norwich out into 'flat' East Anglia had a total vertical rise greater than other comparable length of main line out of London. Moreover, it was plagued by speed restrictions, so it was all the more remarkable that the ten best Britannia-hauled trains in 1951 were 'faster than the ten best trains on the Western Region's perfectly graded Paddington to Bristol run over a comparable distance'. Photograph James Stevenson, courtesy Hamish Stevenson.

70009 ALFRED THE GREAT coming into Stowmarket with an afternoon Liverpool Street-Norwich train in the early 1950s. The Claud, 62605, waits to work the connecting train to Bury St Edmunds. 70009 had a spell on the Southern Region in 1951, a temporary replacement for 70004 on display at the Festival of Britain. It worked with the other SR Britannia, 70014 IRON DUKE from Nine Elms. Photograph Dr Ian C. Allen, The Transport Treasury.

ALFRED again, late on in its GE career, by the famous cab ramp at Liverpool Street in March 1961. It has the modified smoke deflectors and has already acquired the electrification flashes; speedometer fitted and support brackets on the leading and trailing regulator rodding. Photograph A.J. Price, courtesy Frank Hornby.

A 'Brit.' in typical latter-day condition, 70009 – inevitably a Kingmoor engine – without name but in good steaming health – at Barrow in August 1966. Photograph D.W. Winkworth.

70010 OWEN GLENDOWER with the 3.45pm Norwich-Liverpool Street service passing Marks Tey on 21 March 1959. Modified deflectors, smokebox footstep. Photograph Michael Mensing.

OWEN GLENDOWER again, a good 'final condition' example of a Britannia, coming north on the Down Slow at Bushey Troughs, with a freight from Willesden about 1963-64. 70010 had gone to Willesden from the GE Section in March 1963. Photograph J.G. Walmsley, The Transport Treasury.

The old and the new on the Great Eastern. 70011 HOTSPUR hurries by Ipswich shed with the 10 o'clock from Norwich, 4 April 1952. Outside the famously decrepit shed are J15 0-6-0 65430, J17 0-6-0 65560 and L1 2-6-4T 67709. There was truly something of the 'shock of the new' about the Britannias – something this fine view seems to encapsulate. HOTSPUR was one of the Britannias which suffered wheel movement in the 1951 episode – at Hatfield Peverel on 4 September 1951. Photograph H.N. James.

70012 JOHN OF GAUNT looking thoroughly tired at Liverpool Street, August 1959. The dynamometer tests with 70006 mentioned earlier were discontinued once an early problem with the 7Ps manifested itself – a severe fore and aft oscillation between the tender and the leading coach. This was duly sorted out by modifications to the buffering and drawgear but only after it threatened the quality of ride of the well-heeled Golden Arrow patrons (as Cox confessed). Photograph D.H. Beecroft, The Transport Treasury.

The Broadsman, a train we are becoming very familiar with, at Liverpool Street. The picture is not dated but is very early on in 70013 OLIVER CROMWELL's career – probably in 1951, its first year. The first twenty or so Britannias had upright vacuum brake pipes, rising above (like here) the top of the buffer beam. Later engines had pipes that projected forward. The earlier ones were modified accordingly; most were done more or less straight away though others lingered on for a while. OLIVER (2004 will hopefully be its great year) still has fluted rods, the smokebox footstep, no 'flexible screens', no tender footstep and (the clincher) still has the bolted plate cover over the lubricator (follow that drive rod up from the end of the slidebar). Photograph D.H. Beecroft, The Transport Treasury.

70013 OLIVER CROMWELL runs over the Trowse swing bridge at Norwich, 13 August 1953 – the lubricator cover plate has now gone but there's no tender footstep yet. Photograph J. Robertson, The Transport Treasury.

OLIVER at Norwich Thorpe station in August 1958; vacuum brake pipe now projects forward, plain section rods long since fitted, smokebox steps, AWS, second tender totem, LM-style four bolt return crank but, three years after the Milton accident, yet to acquire deflector handhold. The joys of engine picking! Photograph D.W. Winkworth.

OLIVER near the end, now at last (long after anyone remembered why, probably) with deflector handholds and the extra grab at the base, at Stockport Edgeley on 28 April 1968. That front running plate looks bent but is an optical illusion, characteristic at certain angles. Photograph W.G. Royden, courtesy Frank Hornby.

Above. The other Southern favourite, a glittering 70014 IRON DUKE, just a few weeks old, at Surbiton in July 1951 with the 8.30am Waterloo-Bournemouth. Lubricator cover still on. Even the motion (including original fluted rods) shimmers. Photograph A.J. Pike, courtesy Frank Hornby.

Top right. IRON DUKE retained its original 'dangerous' deflector handrails to the end. Here it is at Willesden shed and its famous forest of lamps late on, 26 June 1964. 70014 of course spent much of its time on the Golden Arrow and can be seen so engaged in the front cover illustration. Photograph Peter Groom.

Below right. 70015 APOLLO, the first of the WR 7Ps, arriving at Wembley with a Cup Final special on 7 May 1960. It had come to the LMR in 1958, to Trafford Park for the Midland line workings and from the end of 1960 began a typical series of perambulations around the LM, ending up, equally typically, at Kingmoor. Note WR-style cut-outs on deflector. APOLLO had first been noted out on the road, like most of its GE Section brethren, during 1951 on a favourite running-in working, from Birmingham to Manchester. When the Britannias were being built, Manchester London Road was the best place to see them! Photograph N.L. Browne, courtesy Frank Hornby.

70016 ARIEL leaving Paddington on 29 July 1961. Just as the deflector handrails were deemed obstructive to the driver's forward vision, so was the ejector exhaust and it was accordingly ordered to be lowered. The Western altered all their Britannias (though 70021 at least had it put back in the original position on the LM in the early 1960s) though elsewhere it was not though worthwhile. ARIEL was unusual in that briefly, before arriving on the Western Region, it had been on loan to the LMR, at Leeds Holbeck of all places, for some months from 1951 to 1952. Note the ejector exhaust duly lowered, the deflector cut-outs and on this loco, a short lubricator drive rod – compare with the long ones seen hitherto. Photograph R.C. Riley, The Transport Treasury.

70017 ARROW, one of the Old Oak Britannias concentrated by now (along with the Laira ones) at Cardiff Canton, waits at platform 2, Birmingham Snow Hill with the 5.15pm to Cardiff via Hereford, Sunday 9 March 1958. Photographs Michael Mensing.

In the year of the Milton accident, 70018 FLYING DUTCHMAN with deflector handrails, runs through West Ealing with the 11.55am Paddington-South Wales express, 11 April 1955. Photograph R.C. Riley, The Transport Treasury.

Altered in the light of Milton, the DUTCHMAN on the Capitals United Express at Newport, May 1960. A suitably impressed spotter sinks to his knees. Photograph D.W. Winkworth.

A sad 70019 LIGHTNING amid the sprouting poles and lamps of Willesden shed, 8 July 1964. Beyond all those detail alterations over the years, it still retains one of the first features to be changed – a fluted rear coupling rod. Photograph James Stevenson, courtesy Hamish Stevenson.

A brand new Western Britannia, 70020 MERCURY at Bath Spa with an up stopper, 18 August 1951. The eye of faith can just discern the gubbins of the WR ATC under the buffer. Photograph Ivo Peters, courtesy Julian Peters.

70020 MERCURY, altered in the usual small details, with a down South Wales express in Sonning Cutting, 14 June 1959. MERCURY was the WR Britannia which, inexplicably, got the 'LM' style handholds. The job was presumably done at Crewe; the exhaust ejector, however, would have been lowered at Swindon... Photograph Peter Groom.

Willesden again in the early 1960s with 70021 MORNING STAR; 'NOT TO BE MOVED' signs back and front. The ejector exhaust, if the WR did in fact get round to lowering it, has been restored to its former position. Short lubricator drive rod, brackets to regulator rodding, WR 'sideways' lamp irons gone and LM ones substituted. They are in the rearranged 'under the wires' configuration. The reversed plate on the front is presumably for the paper LM reporting numbers. Photograph J.G. Walmsley, The Transport Treasury.

Top left. 70022 TORNADO rushes past Southall shed with a Cardiff train on 4 April 1959. Photograph Frank Hornby.

Bottom left. The (of course) beautiful 70023 VENUS, at Newport High Street in May 1960, then with a Canton 86C plate. It went to Kingmoor a second time, the last shed in its career, in October 1966. It never got the BR AWS after transfer from the Western. See the next picture for more on that shedplate... Photograph D.W. Winkworth.

Below. An unusual photograph in several historical footnote-ish ways. It's a Western Region engine at Newcastle which is enough to raise an eyebrow in any case, though any Britannia on Tyneside would be worthy of note. It's July 1961 and 70023 VENUS carries an 88A shedplate – the code briefly owned by Canton from September 1960 until it closed to steam two years later. VENUS herself left for Kingmoor in September 1961. Now, let's look at the lamp irons. The smokebox door iron is a 'sideways' WR one, as you'd expect for a WR engine while those on the buffer beam are 'face on' – that is, conventional BR. In the previous picture they are very definitely WR-style. Moreover, 70023 still has irons on the deflector stays, fitted while on loan to the Southern in 1953 when covering for Bulleid Pacifics stopped in the broken axle episode.

70024 VULCAN at Dawlish Warren on 28 August 1954, when still a Laira engine and pretty enough for a BR poster! VULCAN was the subject of a letter in 'Trains Illustrated' in 1961; a Canton engine by then, it was being used exclusively on London diagrams and was running up a GE-style total of nearly 2,500 miles every seven days. Canton, however, preferred its new Kings for the London jobs and such work was restricted to newly-outshopped Britannias only... Photograph R.C. Riley, The Transport Treasury.

30

70025 WESTERN STAR at Highworth Junction with the 8am Cardiff-Paddington train, 14 May 1955. It was the first of Canton's original five Britannias, 70025-70029, going there at the end of 1952. The planned distribution on the Western Region was Canton, Old Oak, Laira though, as is well known, they were all later concentrated in Cardiff, to much better effect. They even got off on a much better footing at Canton than elsewhere on the Western and the shed immediately got them on productive diagrams. Nonetheless without fundamental re-casting they could hardly expect to out-do the home-grown brethren and mileages of the (eventually) fifteen Canton Britannias were hardly distinguishable from the Castles all around them. Photograph R.C. Riley, The Transport Treasury.

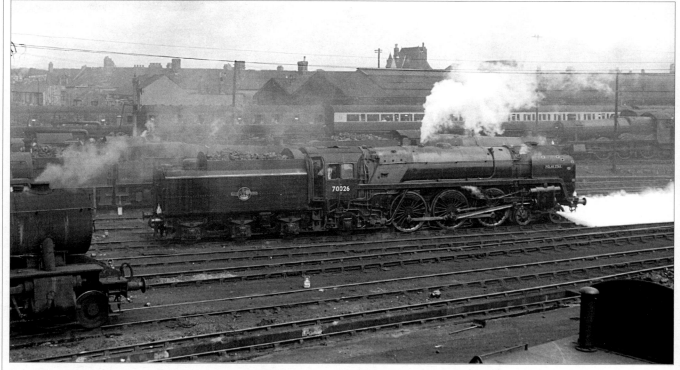

A Heiron Interlude, above and opposite. 70026 POLAR STAR at its Canton home in 1960, readied to work the Capitals United Express. Inconsistencies abounded in the way the deflectors were modified after the Milton accident of 1955 – 70026, the engine involved for instance, emerged after a long spell in works with its handrails at first intact! The only difference was that the inward curvature of the deflectors was slightly modified. Later of course it got the handholes. Note the higher dome on the BR1A tender. Photographs George Heiron, courtesy Mrs Shirley Heiron, The Transport Treasury.

70027 RISING STAR at Cardiff General, 1 June 1953, very much in 'original' condition. Arriving brand new from Swindon in November 1952, within two days it was working The Red Dragon. Photograph R.C. Riley, The Transport Treasury.

70028 ROYAL STAR with a down express at Acton West Junction, 30 June 1956. Photograph R.C. Riley, The Transport Treasury.

ROYAL STAR in very different circumstances, at Crewe in the 1960s with no hint of any lining. Photograph Paul Chancellor Collection.

The last of the Western Region Britannias, 70029 SHOOTING STAR leaving Paddington past the Ranelagh bridge engine yard on 30 August 1958 with the 3.45pm train for the distant west of South Wales. There were unconvincing aspects to the recommendations after the 1955 Milton accident and even the Western, after a while, was hardly frantic in its efforts to modify the deflector handrails and ejector exhaust. Some three years on, while 70029 has got the 1957 second tender totem, the 'pre-Milton' features are still there. Note the short lubricator drive rod. All fifteen WR Britannias ended up at Canton (a much more sensible division than first arrived at) though three did go to the LMR fairly soon. Photograph R.C. Riley, The Transport Treasury.

35

Left and bottom left. 70030 WILLIAM WORDSWORTH at the little coaling plant outside Liverpool Street station, 2 October 1958. 70030 had actually gone new to the London Midland, with 70034; the two airbraked engines, 70043 and 70044, had been intended for the Eastern Region but it was these two which stayed while 70030 and 70034 went east instead. Photograph R.C. Riley, The Transport Treasury.

Below. All too much a latter-day Britannia. Filthy and battered, 70031 BYRON. As pointed out in *The Book of the Britannias*, this was the first true LM Britannia, in the sense that it went there from new and stayed there to withdrawal. AWS, three visible sand filler caps; 70031 is approaching Rugby on 20 July 1962. Photograph The Transport Treasury.

Good honest Longsight Britannia; a platform view of 70032 TENNYSON at Crewe in 1958. The old Manchester shed operated a stud of BR 7Ps through most of the 1950s yet here as elsewhere they proved less than revolutionary. It was the old story – they did not provide obviously greater power than the existing engines (in this case Royal Scots) for the diagrams they were expected to work. In the initial disposition, there were fifteen or so Britannias scattered over the LMR and the ScR, from North Wales to Manchester to Glasgow. It would have been better to have concentrated them all on one shed, together with the Western ones, and work a decent fleet of thirty or so from one or two sheds. Photograph A.H. Lucas, The Transport Treasury.

70033 CHARLES DICKENS approaching Rugby on the Trent Valley line with the up 2pm Manchester/11.50am Colne to Euston train, 29 April 1958. Unusually good view of the three sand filler covers. Photograph Michael Mensing.

70034 THOMAS HARDY at Willesden shed, 10 June 1964. Lamp irons on the deflector stays are a reminder of its days as a loan engine on the Southern for a few weeks in 1953, when the Merchant Navy Pacifics suffered axle problems and were temporarily withdrawn. Photograph James Stevenson, courtesy Hamish Stevenson.

70035 RUDYARD KIPLING at Sleaford in July 1963; it had recently become a March engine and would move on to Kingmoor at the end of the year. In between it had been one of the GE Britannias to go to Immingham for work on the GN to Kings Cross. Photograph D.W. Winkworth.

70036 BOADICEA leaving York on the 12.30pm Newcastle-Colchester on 11 April 1961 – J72 pilot 68736 in NER livery is at work behind. Photograph P.J. Lynch.

70037 HEREWARD THE WAKE on Brentwood Bank, 5 September 1953. To observe the obvious hulking power of a 7P in this period compared to B1s and B17s is to recognise the great advance in power and availability they represented. Observers were flabbergasted when even the first ten 7Ps replaced so many B1 and B17 4-6-0s in 1951 (three SR Bulleid light Pacifics were made available as cover) and gave a greatly improved service to boot. It was just as well that the 4-6-0s were still around in October 1951 when the Britannias were temporarily withdrawn following the various wheel shifting incidents. It was early the next year before all the GE ones got back home from repair at Crewe. The high mileages of the 7Ps was due to inspired diagramming as much as anything else – as well as The Broadsman and others, worked by Stratford and Norwich, Stratford Britannias such as HEREWARD shared in intensive boat train workings to the north of England, manned by Parkeston crews. Photograph R. Wilson, The Transport Treasury.

70038 ROBIN HOOD, one of the Stratford 'Brits.' transferred to Norwich in 1959, on a 'Clacton'. They were put on these difficult and important trains ('to London by Britannia' urged the advertising boards) as dieselisation advanced on the GE. With AWS protector plate prominent, ROBIN HOOD is snaking out of Colchester station with a down train, past the rickety old engine shed. Photograph Dr Ian C. Allen, The Transport Treasury.

There were no shiny new maintenance facilities, despite the 'flag ship' nature of the new GE Britannia fleet and they underwent shed repairs cheek by jowl with the older inhabitants, as perfectly illustrated here at Stratford in the 1950s, ROBIN standing outside the repair shed among the usual tanks, 0-6-0s and so on. Another 'Brit.' stands behind as 70038 undergoes some form of valve work among other things. Note how the lower part of the deflectors come off to gain access to the cylinders. Photograph Dr Ian C. Allen, The Transport Treasury.

70039 SIR CHRISTOPHER WREN approaching Cambridge with a down Liverpool Street train, 27 April 1958. So satisfactorily had the Britannia revolution been wrought that it was marshalled into despairing last ditch arguments against dieselisation. And if you look at the sheer cost of dieselising just *the main lines* in East Anglia (with all those generously appointed specially designed depots – later closed) it is hard not to agree... For instance, the fifteen GE Britannias working the new timetable, BR claimed at the time, saved £50,000 a year. This yielded a return on investment of something like 22% a year, against interest rates then of 4%. How could their replacement by (in large part) Type 3s of *less* power with all the costs of training, new plant and so on, improve on that? Photograph R.C. Riley, The Transport Treasury.

70040 CLIVE OF INDIA pounds out of the tunnel at Ipswich heading south past the engine shed (the beginnings of it are on the right) on 22 May 1957. The great advantage of the Britannias was that, not only were they so demonstrably at home with express passenger work, as here, but they could (this was an underlying principle all across the BR Standard range) work almost anything else, from fast freight to stopping passenger. The secret was that wondrous boiler, which could make steam efficiently almost whatever the job. Photograph R.C. Riley, The Transport Treasury.

A somewhat changed CLIVE OF INDIA at Grimsby, soon after arrival at Immingham shed, in 1960. They would replace B1s, repeating a trick from 1951 though it did not work so well this time around. They were not new engines by any means, for a start, and were limited in number. Nevertheless the crews were won over more or less straight away. Even though failures were experienced *power* was the key – they had long been famed for their reserves of steam even on the best of the Norwich line schedules. This is probably not the best picture to introduce it, but 70040-70049 had plain bearings on the rear truck – you can just see the way the axle box cover (here with its oil pipe) differs from the Timken ones seen so far... Photograph The Transport Treasury.

70041 SIR JOHN MOORE passing Trowse Lower Junction box (the sign on the brickwork reads NORWICH 1 MILE with an arrow pointing to the right – don't you just miss those signs?) Photograph J. Robertson, The Transport Treasury.

70041 SIR JOHN MOORE at Kings Cross about 1962. Against all expectations, redundant GE Section Britannias had found themselves on the already Pacific-rich Great Northern from 1960, replacing B1s on the Cleethorpes trains. The first three to go to Immingham for these jobs were 70039, 70040 and 70041 at the end of 1960 and though not in the best of nick it was possible to accelerate a couple of Grimsby expresses. By autumn 1961 seven were available and the characteristic white smokebox door straps and dart were everyday sights at Kings Cross. Photograph The Transport Treasury.

70042 LORD ROBERTS at Norwich Thorpe on 2 September 1955, at the height of the Britannias' reign in East Anglia. It has the plain bearing rear truck, though the reader might need to take our word for it; just about visible is the vertical lubrication pipe, later removed. Photograph Peter Groom.

LORD ROBERTS again, now an LMR engine, at Willesden shed on 17 April 1962. Several features are worth looking at... Take the Timken roller bearing rear truck, instantly recognisable from the red band across the yellow casing (a late livery feature). 70042 was of course one of the ten (70040-70049) with plain bearing rear trucks but through some chance at a works visit it subsequently got this roller bearing one. There must have been spares, for no former roller bearing Britannia has turned up with a plain bearing rear truck. LORD ROBERTS turns out to be perfectly suited to engine picking; it retained its deflector handrails to the end, the usual 7 above the number was (uniquely) 'upgraded' to 7P and all three 'GE' buffer beam lamp irons have been altered, to a hybrid arrangement of two 'medium' ones with a small one in between. Look at the support for the smokebox door footstep compared with the previous picture, and compare the length of the lubricator drive rods. Joy! Photograph Peter Groom.

It was decided to turn out the final pair of the 1953 programme, 70043 and 70044, with Westinghouse air brakes for a variety of tests. These included double heading 1,500 ton trains on the traditional testing ground, Toton-Brent – and a staggering sight they must have been in 1953. The gear was removed in 1957 and the two became conventional Britannias. Both were at Longsight for most of the 1950s apart from spells at Toton and Derby for various tests and trials – 70043 is at Derby during one of these periods, on 10 September 1954. R.J. Buckley, Initial Photographics.

The other Westinghouse engine, 70044 out on the road working the down Euston-Bacup and Colne express at Bourne End on 30 July 1955. In between tests this is what the pair did for most of the time, working Longsight duties ('The Mancunian' was a favourite in the mid-1950s) on the West Coast route. As mentioned earlier, the pair were destined for the GE but the air brake project saw them diverted to the LM; two of Longsight's earlier five, 70030 and 70034, thus went to the GE in their place. Photograph Philip J. Kelley.

Now a conventional Britannia (some trace, a bolt hole or errant stud, must have remained to tell of the air brake episode but sadly for engine pickers these have not been identified) 70044 now EARL HAIG, at Dumfries on 13 June 1959 with the 4pm St Enoch-Leeds. Driver's name bracket on side of cab. A different view of this engine and train is in *The Book of the Britannias*. It was by this time at Holbeck, and thus an NER engine. Photograph James Stevenson, courtesy Hamish Stevenson.

70045 formerly LORD ROWALLAN, the first to feature here with the BR1D coal pusher tender, at Carlisle in August 1966. These last ten, 70045-70054, had speedometer and both regulator rodding brackets from new. This was the Britannia which, uniquely, got oval buffers, in 1966. Photograph D.W. Winkworth.

Of the last ten with the BR1D tenders the first five, 70045-70049, went new to Holyhead for Irish Mails and other trains. This is 70046 ANZAC near Bushey on the LNW main line in the 1950s. It stayed on the London Midland throughout its life, though it strayed to former Western turf at Banbury for a few months and former Scottish Region territory at, inevitably, Kingmoor.

The Curious Case of the Britannia With No Name. 70047 on a Manchester-Euston express between Berkswell and Beechwood tunnels (on the Birmingham-Coventry route), Sunday 25 June 1961. It affords a glimpse at least of the coal pusher at the rear of the BR1D tender. Photograph Michael Mensing.

70048 THE TERRITORIAL ARMY 1908-1958 in beautiful ex-works condition at Crewe on 8 November 1959. This can be considered the 'final' condition for the Britannias – AWS, speedometer, BR1D tender – if any more had been built, though how the deflectors would have looked is anyone's guess. Here is 70048, ex-works more than four years after Milton still with the offending handrails (they were never modified on 70048 in fact). Thirty-six more Britannias were proposed and then cancelled, so the last would have been numbered 70090... Photograph Alec Swain, The Transport Treasury.

70049 as yet not named, at Chester on one of its North Wales jobs, in August 1955. Photograph D.W. Winkworth.

And at last one of the Holyhead 'Brits.' with The Irish Mail headboard up, 70049 at Holyhead shed in the 1950s. It was the last to be named, in May 1960, SOLWAY FIRTH. It was an accidental choice of name; the Scottish 'Brits.', 70050-70054 were named after Firths because they would be working in Scotland and 70049 was left so late someone just picked a Firth for the sake of tidiness. Photograph A. Scarsbrook, Initial Photographics.

70050 FIRTH OF CLYDE, a Crewe North engine by this time, at Willesden on 6 October 1963. Like all the Britannias, eventually even the Firths had to go to England. In truth they had not made much of an impression on the Scottish Region and it is difficult to see how they could. All Polmadie did was slot them into Royal Scot diagrams where they would be less sure-footed and certainly no more powerful, or some Pacific jobs where they would never be considered up to the task. Or they would work in place of Jubilees. Spares would be awkward and crews might only come across one every few months. For much of the time the nearest Britannias to the Polmadie stud were in Manchester – and they worked south! Photograph Frank Hornby.

70051 FIRTH OF FORTH on a typical Polmadie job, a Birmingham to Glasgow train at Golborne on 23 August 1957. Polmadie could not really find enough to do for its five Britannias (what a sad contrast to the GE) and all went to the LMR at the end of 1962 – two in fact, 70053 and 70054, the ScR had got rid of even earlier, to Leeds Holbeck. So for half the time the ScR only had *three* Britannias! Typical duties would involve jobs deep into England, to Birmingham, Crewe or Manchester and one would be found on layover at sheds like Newton Heath – see 70052 in *The Book of the Britannias* for instance. This sort of proved the point about the way Polmadie was forced to find work its Britannias – such duties were Jubilee territory or, in the 1950s, the Class 6 Clans. Photograph Les Elsey.

70052 FIRTH OF TAY leaving Glasgow St Enoch with the 8pm 'Starlight Special' on 13 July 1962. A good look at the rear of the BR1D tender with coal pusher equipment; behind the train is the old St Enoch engine shed. Photograph James Stevenson, courtesy Hamish Stevenson.

70053 MORAY FIRTH at Crewe Works, 8 November 1964 – a recent repaint in plain green. It was one of the two which went to Holbeck before the LMR, eventually finding itself briefly at Holyhead from 1964 to 1965. Photograph Alec Swain, The Transport Treasury.

70054 DORNOCH FIRTH at Polmadie about 1956. For once it can be seen how the sand boxes disposed the sand (this was the second arrangement remember): rear one to front of rear driver and rear of middle driver, middle one to front of the centre driver and front one to the front of the leading driver. Photograph J. Paterson, The Transport Treasury.

Glorious finale. DORNOCH FIRTH on Beattock, 16 July 1955. Photograph J. Robertson, The Transport Treasury.